Trash–Free Lunch Day

Focus: Pollution

Meredith Costain

The trash cans at our school are often full.

The trash cans are filled with food wrappers and metal cans. Sometimes the wind blows the trash around the playground.

We wanted to have less litter on our playground, so we tried an experiment.

First we had to find out
how much trash we made
in one day.

We collected the trash
from all of the cans
around the school.

Then we weighed the trash.
We wrote down our results.

Next we had a Trash-Free Lunch Day.

Everyone brought a trash-free lunch to school. No paper bags. No plastic wrappers. No metal cans.

Some kids brought sandwiches in lunch boxes. Lunch boxes can be used again.

Some kids brought drinks
in bottles.
Bottles can be used again.

Some kids brought fruit.
Fruit has its own wrapper.

At the end of lunch,
we collected the trash.
We weighed the trash.
We wrote down our results.

Then we compared
the results.

Which day do you think had the most trash?

Glossary

collected   gathered

compared   looked to see how things are the same or how they are different

experiment a test to find something out

results   the outcome of the test

weighed   found out how heavy something is

wrapper   a cover